BY M. J. YORK • ILLUSTRATED BY KATHLEEN PETELINSEK

Published by The Child's World®
1980 Lookout Drive • Mankato, MN 56003-1705
800-599-READ • www.childsworld.com

Acknowledgments
The Child's World®: Mary Berendes, Publishing Director
Translator: Dr. Susanne M. Wagner, Assistant Professor of
German & Program Director, University of St. Thomas
The Design Lab: Design
Red Line Editorial: Editorial direction
Amnet: Production

ISBN 9781626873759
LCCN 2014930646

Printed in the United States of America
Mankato, MN
July, 2014
PA02217

9683

## ABOUT THE AUTHOR

M. J. York is a children's author and editor living in Minnesota. She loves learning about different people and places.

## ABOUT THE ILLUSTRATOR

Kathleen Petelinsek loves to draw and paint. She also loves to travel to exotic countries where people speak foreign languages. She lives in Minnesota with her husband, two daughters, two dogs, a fluffy cat, and three chickens.

# CONTENTS

# Introduction to German

German is spoken in Germany, Austria, and Switzerland. It has the sixth-most speakers of any world language. More than 90 million people speak German as their first language.

German is related to English and Dutch. People spoke ancient German more than 2,000 years ago. Today, written German is the same everywhere. But spoken German can sound very different.

The German alphabet has the same 26 letters as the English alphabet. It also has four more letters of its own. The dots over the three vowels, ä, ö, and ü, are called an umlaut.

**ä** makes a sound between *eh* and *ay* as in *say*

**ö** makes a sound between *eu* and the *u* in *burn*

**ü** makes a sound like an *ue* said with your mouth shaped like an *o*

The fourth letter, ß, is called "ess tsett." It is like a double *ss* or an *s* with more hissing.

And some letters are said differently than in English:

**h**   usually makes the vowel it follows longer

**w**   sounds like v in vote

**v**   sounds like f in found

**s**   usually sounds like z in zebra

**ei**   sounds like eye

**ie**   sounds like ee

In German, there are no silent letters. All the letters are pronounced, even an e at the end of a word. A double consonant usually makes the vowel it follows shorter. Usually the first syllable is stressed.

German nouns are always capitalized, just like English proper nouns. All other words are only capitalized when at the beginning of the sentence.

# My Home
# Mein Haus
*(mine hauws)*

window
**das Fenster**
*(dahs fenn-ster)*

lamp
**die Lampe**
*(dee lahm-puh)*

bathroom
**das Badezimmer**
*(dahs bahd-uh-tsim-mer)*

bedroom
**das Schlafzimmer**
*(dahs shlaf-tsim-mer)*

television
**der Fernseher**
*(dare fern-zay-er)*

kitchen
**die Küche**
*(dee kue-sha)*

cat
**die Katze**
*(dee kah-tsuh)*

living room
**das Wohnzimmer**
*(dahs vone-tsim-mer)*

sofa
**das Sofa**
*(dahs zoh-fah)*

chair
**der Stuhl**
*(dare shtool)*

table
**der Tisch**
*(dare tish)*

# In the Morning
# Am Morgen
*(ahm mor-gin)*

dresser
**die Kommode**
*(dee ko-MOH-duh)*

clock
**die Uhr**
*(dee oor)*

teddy bear
**der Teddybär**
*(dare ted-e-bayre)*

doll
**die Puppe**
*(dee poo-puh)*

pillow
**das Kissen**
*(dahs kiss-in)*

bed
**das Bett**
*(dahs bet)*

blanket
**die Decke**
*(dee deck-uh)*

comb
**der Kamm**
*(dare kahm)*

Good morning! It is seven o'clock.
**Guten Morgen!**
**Es ist sieben Uhr.**
*(goot-en mor-gin!*
*es ist zee-bin oor.)*

brush
**die Bürste**
*(dee buer-stuh)*

closet
**der Schrank**
*(dare shrahngk)*

shirt
**das Hemd**
*(dahs hemdt)*

I feel awake.
**Ich bin wach.**
*(ikh bin vahkh.)*

**MORE USEFUL WORDS**
I feel tired.
**Ich bin müde.**
*(ikh bin mue-duh.)*

I feel happy.
**Ich bin glücklich.**
*(ikh bin gluek-leekh.)*

dress
**das Kleid**
*(dahs klide)*

skirt
**der Rock**
*(dare rohk)*

pants
**die Hose**
*(dee ho-zuh)*

socks
**die Socken**
*(dee zock-en)*

shoes
**die Schuhe**
*(dee shoo-uh)*

# At the Park
# Im Park
*(im park)*

Let's play!
**Lasst uns spielen!**
*(Lahst oons shpeel-in!)*

sky
**der Himmel**
*(dare him-uhl)*

friend (masculine)
**der Freund**
*(dare froyndt)*

friend (feminine)
**die Freundin**
*(dee froyn-din)*

bird
**der Vogel**
*(dare foh-guhl)*

soccer ball
**der Fußball**
*(dare foos-ball)*

## MORE USEFUL WORDS

game
**das Spiel**
*(dahs shpeel)*

sports
**der Sport**
*(dare shport)*

sun
**die Sonne**
*(dee zohn-uh)*

swing
**die Schaukel**
*(dee shauw-kul)*

clouds
**die Wolke**
*(dee vol-kuh)*

playground
**der Spielplatz**
*(dare shpeel-plahts)*

slide
**die Rutsche**
*(dee root-shuh)*

water
**das Wasser**
*(dahs vahs-er)*

pond
**der See**
*(dare zee)*

flower
**die Blume**
*(dee bloo-muh)*

duck
**die Ente**
*(dee en-tuh)*

13

airplane
**das Flugzeug**
*(dahs floogk-tsoygh)*

office
**das Büro**
*(dahs bue-roh)*

building
**das Gebäude**
*(dahs geh-BOY-duh)*

bus
**der Bus**
*(dare boos)*

CITY BUS

**MORE USEFUL WORDS**

truck
**der Lastwagen**
*(dare lahst-vah-gin)*

train
**der Zug**
*(dare tsoogh)*

stop
**Stopp**
*(shtohp)*

go
**Los**
*(lohs)*

police officer (feminine)
**die Polizistin**
*(dare poh-liht-zhist-in)*

firefighter (masculine)
**der Feuerwehrmann**
*(dare foy-yer-vehr-mahn)*

# My Birthday Party
## Meine
## Geburtstagsfeier
*(mine-uh geh-burts-tahgs-fyre)*

### MORE USEFUL WORDS

| | |
|---|---|
| one<br>**eins**<br>*(ines)* | eleven<br>**elf**<br>*(elf)* |
| two<br>**zwei**<br>*(tsvigh)* | twelve<br>**zwölf**<br>*(tsvuhlf)* |
| three<br>**drei**<br>*(drigh)* | thirteen<br>**dreizehn**<br>*(drigh-tsayn)* |
| four<br>**vier**<br>*(feer)* | fourteen<br>**vierzehn**<br>*(feer-tsayn)* |
| five<br>**fünf**<br>*(fuenf)* | fifteen<br>**fünfzehn**<br>*(fuenf-tsayn)* |
| six<br>**sechs**<br>*(zekhs)* | sixteen<br>**sechzehn**<br>*(zekh-tsayn)* |
| seven<br>**sieben**<br>*(zee-bin)* | seventeen<br>**siebzehn**<br>*(zeeb-tsayn)* |
| eight<br>**acht**<br>*(ahkht)* | eighteen<br>**achtzehn**<br>*(ahkh-tsayn)* |
| nine<br>**neun**<br>*(noyn)* | nineteen<br>**neunzehn**<br>*(noyn-tsayn)* |
| ten<br>**zehn**<br>*(tsayn)* | twenty<br>**zwanzig**<br>*(tzvahn-tsikh)* |

grandmother
**die Großmutter**
*(dee gross-moo-tehr)*

I am six years old.
Ich bin sechs Jahre alt.
*(ihk bin zekhs yah-ruh ahlt.)*

grandfather
**der Großvater**
*(dare gross-fah-tehr)*

brother
**der Bruder**
*(dare broo-dehr)*

sister
**die Schwester**
*(dee shves-tehr)*

cake
**der Kuchen**
*(dare kookh-in)*

19

# Time for Dinner
## das Abendessen
*(dahs ah-bin-des-in)*

bread
**das Brot**
*(dahs broht)*

stove
**der Herd**
*(dare hayrd)*

pot
**der Topf**
*(dare tohpf)*

I am hungry.
**Ich habe Hunger.**
*(ikh hah-buh hoon-gehr.)*

glass
**das Glas**
*(dahs glahs)*

rice
**der Reis**
*(dare rys)*

meat
**das Fleisch**
*(dahs flighsh)*

plate
**der Teller**
*(dare teh-lehr)*

fork
**die Gabel**
*(dee gah-buhl)*

knife
**das Messer**
*(dahs mess-ehr)*

spoon
**der Löffel**
*(dare luh-fuhl)*

# At Night
# In der Nacht
*(In dare Nahkt)*

Today is Friday.
**Heute ist Freitag.**
*(hoy-tuh isst fry-tahg.)*

Yesterday was Thursday.
**Gestern war Donnerstag.**
*(geh-sturn vahr doh-ners-tahg.)*

Tomorrow is Saturday.
**Morgen ist Samstag.**
*(mor-gin ist zahms-tahg.)*

Good night!
**Gute Nacht!**
*(goo-tuh nahkht!)*

bathtub
**die Badewanne**
*(dee bah-duh-van-uh)*

I am tired!
**Ich bin müde!**
*(ihk bin mue-duh!)*

# MORE USEFUL WORDS

Yes
**Ja**
*(yah)*

No
**Nein**
*(nine)*

ten
**Zehn**
*(tsayn)*

twenty
**Zwanzig**
*(tzvahn-tsikh)*

thirty
**Dreißig**
*(dry-sikh)*

forty
**Vierzig**
*(feer-tsikh)*

fifty
**Fünfzig**
*(fuenf-tsikh)*

sixty
**Sechzig**
*(zekh-tsikh)*

seventy
**Siebzig**
*(zeeb-tsikh)*

eighty
**Achtzig**
*(ahkh-tsikh)*

ninety
**Neunzig**
*(noyn-tsikh)*

one hundred
**Einhundert**
*(ine-hoon-dehrt)*

January
**der Januar**
*(dare yah-noo-ar)*

February
**der Februar**
*(dare feh-broo-ar)*

March
**der März**
*(dare mehrts)*

April
**der April**
*(dare ah-pril)*

May
**der Mai**
*(dare my)*

June
**der Juni**
*(dare yoo-nee)*

July
**der Juli**
*(dare yoo-lee)*

August
**der August**
*(dare auw-goost)*

September
**der September**
*(dare zehp-TEHM-behr)*

October
**der Oktober**
*(dare ok-TOH-behr)*

November
**der November**
*(dare no-VEHM-behr)*

December
**der Dezember**
*(dare deh-TSEM-behr)*

winter
**der Winter**
*(dare vin-tehr)*

spring
**der Frühling**
*(dare frue-ling)*

summer
**der Sommer**
*(dare zom-mehr)*

fall
**der Herbst**
*(dare hehrbst)*

good-bye!
**Auf Wiedersehen!**
*(auwf vee-dare-zayn!)*